HAUNTED AMERICA

Ghosts of
GETTYSBURG
AND OTHER HAUNTINGS OF THE EAST

by Suzanne Garbe

CAPSTONE PRESS
a capstone imprint

Edge Books are published by Capstone Press,
1710 Roe Crest Drive, North Mankato, Minnesota 56003
www.capstonepub.com

Library of Congress Cataloging-in-Publication Data
Garbe, Suzanne.
  Ghosts of Gettysburg and other hauntings of the East / by Suzanne Garbe.
    pages cm.—(Edge Books. Haunted America)
  Includes bibliographical references and index.
  Summary: "Describes ghost sightings and hauntings in the eastern United States"—
Provided by publisher.
  ISBN 978-1-4765-3916-4 (library binding)
  ISBN 978-1-4765-5964-3 (ebook pdf)
1. Haunted places—East (U.S.)—Juvenile literature. 2. Ghosts—East (U.S.)—Juvenile
literature. I. Title.
  BF1472.U6.G3555 2014
  133.10974—dc23   2013031838

Editorial Credits
Anthony Wacholtz, editor; Heidi Thompson, designer; Svetlana Zhurkin,
media researcher; Danielle Ceminsky, production specialist

Photo Credits
Alamy: North Wind Picture Archives, 14; AP Photo: Patrick Semansky, 5, Robert F.
Bukaty, 17; Corbis: Bettmann, 10–11, Roman Soumar, 20 (inset), Star Ledger/Robert
Sciarrino, 22–23; Dreamstime: Wangkun Jia, 18–19; Governor Sprague Mansion
Museum, Cranston Historical Society, Cranston, RI, photo by Gregg A. Mierka, Artist/
Historian, 26–27, 27 (inset); iStockphotos: ilustro, cover (middle); Library of Congress,
6–7, 13 (inset), 15 (top), 20–21, 24–25; Newscom: KRT, 10 (inset); Shutterstock: Dmitry
Natashin (frame), 7, 10, 13, 15, echo3005 (gate), back cover, 2, 30, 32, Ivakoleva
(texture), throughout, Kelleher Photography, 8–9, Map Resources, 28, Nagel
Photography, cover (bottom), 1 (front), nikkytok (smoke), throughout, Triff, cover
(top), 1 (back), Victorian Traditions, 7 (top), Zack Frank, 29; Svetlana Zhurkin, 12–13

Direct Quotations
Page 15: Jeff Belanger. "The World's Most Haunted Places." Rev. ed. Pompton Plains,
  N.J.: New Page Book, 2011, 108.
  Page 17: http://hauntedlights.com/haunted1.html
  Page 25: Michael Norman and Beth Scott. "Haunted America." New York: TOR,
  1994, 133–134.

Printed in the United States of America in Stevens Point, Wisconsin.
092013   007768WZS14

TABLE OF CONTENTS

The eastern part of the United States is home to our country's oldest buildings and oldest recorded history. So it's not surprising that it's also home to some of our country's most haunted places. Scientists haven't been able to explain or prove the existence of **ghosts**. However, people throughout history have claimed to see ghosts and experience unexplained events. Get ready for a spine-tingling tour of some of the most haunted places of the East.

WESTMINSTER BURYING GROUNDS

One place said to be haunted is the Westminster Burying Grounds in Baltimore, Maryland. The famous American writer Edgar Allan Poe was buried there in 1849. Poe was known for his mysterious and creepy stories. After Poe died, people believed his ghost came back to haunt them. According to legend, Poe's ghost has been seen near his burial site. It has also been spotted in the **catacombs** beneath the cemetery.

Poe isn't the only ghost said to haunt Westminster. Visitors to the burying grounds have heard unseen children playing and seen a mysterious man in a gray vest. People claiming to be **mediums** have also heard a man yelling, "Go away!"

CITY: Baltimore, Maryland

FIRST REPORTED HAUNTING: unknown

TYPES OF ACTIVITY: ghost sightings, voices

SCARY RANKING: 2

ACCESS: Open to the public. Guided tours available, including a Halloween tour.

ORIGINAL BURIAL PLACE OF

EDGAR ALLAN POE

FROM

OCTOBER 9, 1849.

UNTIL

NOVEMBER 17, 1875.

MRS. MARIA CLEMM HIS MOTHER-IN-LAW
LIES UPON HIS RIGHT AND VIRGINIA POE
HIS WIFE UPON HIS LEFT UNDER TH
MONUMENT ERECTED TO HIM IN TH

ghost—a spirit of a dead person believed to haunt people or places

catacomb—an underground cemetery

medium—a person who claims to communicate with the spirit world

GETTYSBURG BATTLEFIELD

The deadliest battle of the Civil War (1861–1865) happened in Gettysburg, Pennsylvania. As the **Union** and **Confederacy** clashed, more than 50,000 soldiers lost their lives over three days. The battle at Gettysburg was a blow to the South. Some people say soldiers who took part in the battle of Gettysburg still roam the battlefield.

CITY: Gettysburg, Pennsylvania

FIRST REPORTED HAUNTING: 1863

TYPES OF ACTIVITY: ghost sightings, strange smells, sounds such as footsteps and voices

SCARY RANKING: 5

ACCESS: The park is free and open to the public. Several private companies operate ghost tours.

Gettysburg has a long history of reported hauntings. The first one happened during the battle itself in 1863. During the battle, troops from Maine arrived outside of Gettysburg to support the Union. However, they weren't sure where to go. At a fork in the road, a man riding a horse and wearing a tri-cornered hat appeared. Hundreds of soldiers and several officers all said the figure had the face of George Washington. At the time, though, Washington had been dead for more than 60 years. Although startled, the troops followed Washington's directions. They arrived in time to help push back General Robert E. Lee's Confederate forces.

George Washington

Union—the northern states that fought against the southern
   states in the Civil War
Confederacy—the 11 southern states that left the United States
   to form the Confederate States of America

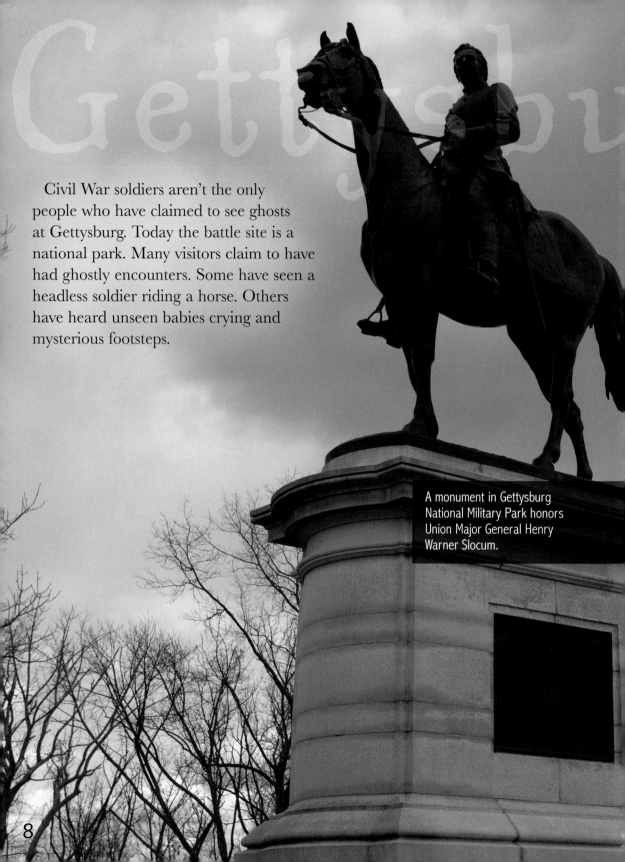

Civil War soldiers aren't the only people who have claimed to see ghosts at Gettysburg. Today the battle site is a national park. Many visitors claim to have had ghostly encounters. Some have seen a headless soldier riding a horse. Others have heard unseen babies crying and mysterious footsteps.

A monument in Gettysburg National Military Park honors Union Major General Henry Warner Slocum.

Some people think ghosts are reliving battle scenes of the war. Visitors have heard gunfire, running horses, and the heavy booms of cannon fire.

In one building during the war, injured soldiers' limbs were amputated and thrown out a window. Today a window in that building vibrates loudly.

One soldier is said to have haunted the cemetery for years. He was supposedly upset that his tombstone didn't mention the Medal of Honor he'd won. As soon as the marking was changed to include the medal, his ghost wasn't seen again.

LIZZIE BORDEN HOUSE

On August 4, 1892, the bodies of Andrew and Abby Borden were discovered in their home. Police thought they had been killed with an axe. Andrew's daughter, Lizzie, was accused of their murder. A jury found her not guilty, but people continue to debate whether or not she committed the murders.

Lizzie Borden

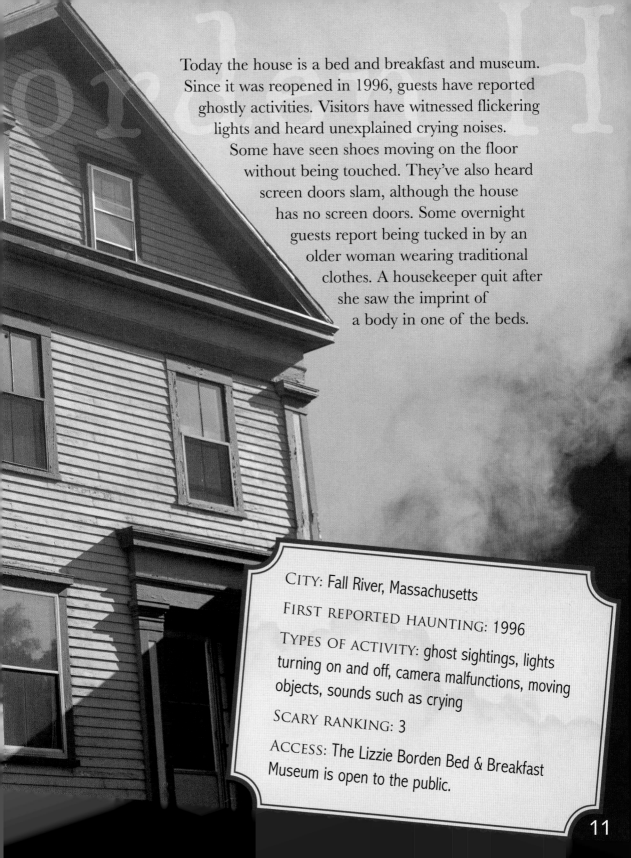

Today the house is a bed and breakfast and museum. Since it was reopened in 1996, guests have reported ghostly activities. Visitors have witnessed flickering lights and heard unexplained crying noises. Some have seen shoes moving on the floor without being touched. They've also heard screen doors slam, although the house has no screen doors. Some overnight guests report being tucked in by an older woman wearing traditional clothes. A housekeeper quit after she saw the imprint of a body in one of the beds.

CITY: Fall River, Massachusetts

FIRST REPORTED HAUNTING: 1996

TYPES OF ACTIVITY: ghost sightings, lights turning on and off, camera malfunctions, moving objects, sounds such as crying

SCARY RANKING: 3

ACCESS: The Lizzie Borden Bed & Breakfast Museum is open to the public.

THE WHITE HOUSE

CITY: Washington, D.C.

FIRST REPORTED HAUNTING: between 1852 and 1865

TYPES OF ACTIVITY: ghost sightings, footsteps, cold spots, strange smells, lights turning on and off

ACCESS: Free public tours are sometimes available.

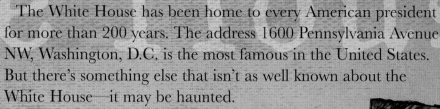
The White House has been home to every American president for more than 200 years. The address 1600 Pennsylvania Avenue NW, Washington, D.C. is the most famous in the United States. But there's something else that isn't as well known about the White House—it may be haunted.

The first ghost reported in the White House was William Lincoln, Abraham Lincoln's son. William died of an illness in 1862. Abraham Lincoln's wife, Mary Todd Lincoln, claimed she saw the ghost of her son every night. He would stand at the foot of her bed and smile at her. Sometimes he came with other family members who had also died. Mary Lincoln told her half sister that seeing William's ghost comforted her.

William Lincoln

However, not every White House ghost is as gentle. Some visitors have reported seeing the ghost of a British soldier carrying a torch. One couple said the ghost tried to set fire to their bed. Ghost hunters think it could be the ghost of one of the soldiers who burned down the White House during the War of 1812.

Dolley Madison's ghost is also said to roam the White House. The wife of President James Madison, Dolley was in charge of planting the White House's famous rose garden. One hundred years later, while Woodrow Wilson was president, gardeners were ordered to dig up the garden. According to legend, Dolley's angry ghost stopped the gardeners.

Dolley Madison

Other ghosts people have seen at the White House include former presidents Abraham Lincoln, William Henry Harrison, and Andrew Jackson. President John Adams' wife, Abigail Adams, has been seen hanging laundry in the East Room. Some people have said they could smell soap and wet clothes.

"When I turned the light on one morning, he [Abraham Lincoln] was sitting there outside his office with his hands over top of each other, legs crossed ... And when I blinked, he was gone."
– Tony Savoy, White House Operations Foreman

15

SEGUIN ISLAND LIGHTHOUSE

In the mid-1800s, a lighthouse keeper lived on Seguin Island, Maine, with his wife. His job was to keep the kerosene lamp lit so ships wouldn't crash into the land. The keeper and his wife lived alone on the small island. To keep his wife from getting bored during the long winter, the keeper bought her a piano. However, the piano had come with only one piece of music. The woman played it over and over, sometimes for hours at a time. Legend has it that the keeper was slowly driven crazy by the music. He took an ax and hacked at the piano. He then killed his wife and himself.

One hundred years later, lighthouse keepers began reporting eerie happenings. They saw doors slam and furniture move on its own. Some visitors claimed to hear the sounds of a piano playing in the distance.

In 1985 new technology allowed the lighthouse to run without a keeper living there. A crew came to clean out the house and remove the furniture. One crew member saw a woman's ghost appear at night. The woman said, "Don't take the furniture. Please leave my home alone!" The next day, they loaded the furniture onto the boat anyway. After everything was loaded, the engine suddenly stopped. The chain keeping the boat in place broke, and the boat sank.

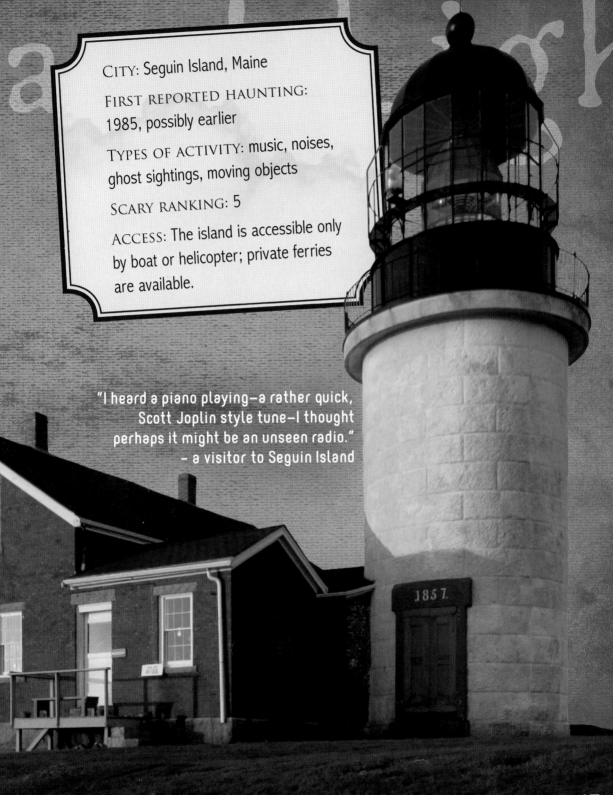

CITY: Seguin Island, Maine

FIRST REPORTED HAUNTING: 1985, possibly earlier

TYPES OF ACTIVITY: music, noises, ghost sightings, moving objects

SCARY RANKING: 5

ACCESS: The island is accessible only by boat or helicopter; private ferries are available.

"I heard a piano playing—a rather quick, Scott Joplin style tune—I thought perhaps it might be an unseen radio."
– a visitor to Seguin Island

OMNI PARKER HOUSE

CITY: Boston, Massachusetts

FIRST REPORTED HAUNTING: 1941, possibly earlier

TYPES OF ACTIVITY: ghost sightings, moving objects, **orbs**, noises

SCARY RANKING: 3

ACCESS: The house is open to the public as a hotel and restaurant.

Guests and staff at the Omni Parker House hotel have reported strange happenings for more than 70 years. Guests have claimed to hear the creaking of a rocking chair, but the hotel doesn't have rocking chairs. A security guard once saw a shadowy figure in a stovepipe hat. Some guests claim the elevators go to the third floor without being called. Staff have also claimed to see orbs floating through the 10th floor hallway.

Harvey Parker, who opened the hotel in 1855, is the most widely reported ghost at the hotel. He worked hard to make sure his guests had an outstanding experience at the hotel and restaurant. Long after Parker died, his ghost was spotted on the 10th floor. Some hotel staff believe Parker stayed behind to make sure guests have a wonderful experience.

orb—a glowing ball of light that sometimes appears at a reportedly haunted location

COLONIAL WILLIAMSBURG

Williamsburg was founded in 1699 as the capital of Virginia. The city grew over time, but Colonial Williamsburg still exists. The historic area lies in the eastern part of the city. Some of the original buildings are still standing today, while others have been rebuilt. Some of the buildings, such as the Peyton Randolph House, are known for their ghostly history.

Peyton Randolph helped lead the Revolutionary War (1775–1783). He **inherited** his father's house, which was later named the Peyton Randolph House. Today the building is open to the public. Employees and guests have seen ghosts of women, men, and children in colonial clothing. The figures have disappeared right before the visitors' eyes. A woman who lived in the house in the mid-1900s also reported strange events. She claimed to hear footsteps and see the ghost of a teenage girl.

Raleigh Tavern is another site in Williamsburg where unexplained events have occurred. The tavern hosted dinners and parties for many people, including George Washington. Visitors to the tavern have heard the sounds of parties when no parties were happening. They have also smelled pipe tobacco when no one is seen smoking.

Raleigh Tavern

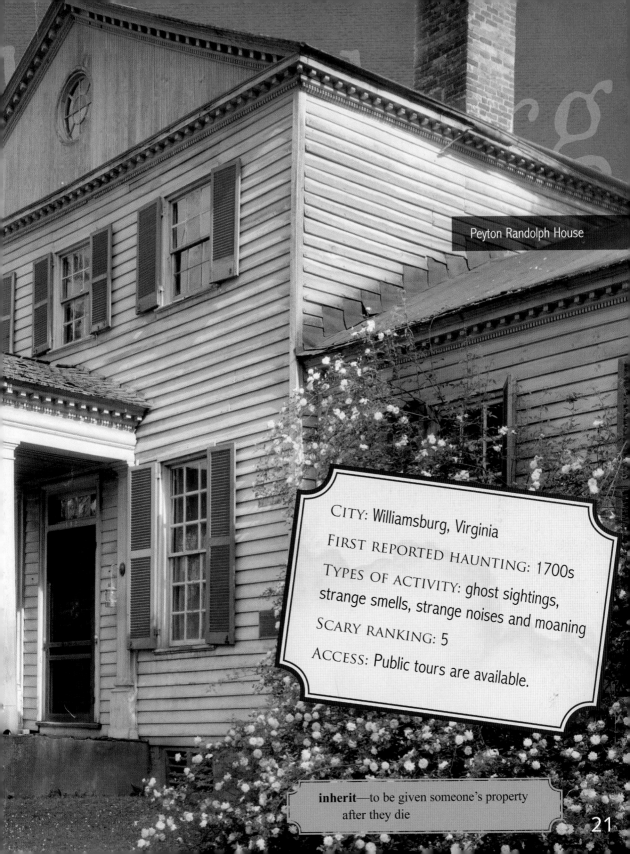

Peyton Randolph House

CITY: Williamsburg, Virginia

FIRST REPORTED HAUNTING: 1700s

TYPES OF ACTIVITY: ghost sightings, strange smells, strange noises and moaning

SCARY RANKING: 5

ACCESS: Public tours are available.

inherit—to be given someone's property after they die

DANVERS STATE HOSPITAL

Danvers State Hospital was built in the 1870s to care for the mentally ill. The hospital grew to include more than 40 buildings. It was built to hold 600 patients, but by 1945 it had as many as 2,360 patients. Not much was known then about treating mental illness. Harsh methods were used to keep the patients under control. Some people believe this treatment led the ghosts of the hospital's patients to haunt the property today.

The 2001 horror film *Session 9* was filmed at Danvers State Hospital before the building was torn down.

Jeralyn Levasseur grew up on the property. Her father was the hospital administrator. She remembers unexplained footsteps in their house, lights flickering, and doors opening and closing on their own. One day she saw the ghost of a woman in the attic. Another day the covers on her bed were pulled off when no one else was in the room.

Stories like Levasseur's drew ghost hunters and tourists to Danvers after the hospital closed in 1992. Many visitors left believing the building was haunted. Today most of the former hospital has been torn down. The only buildings that remain have been turned into luxury apartments, leaving the hauntings of Danvers State Hospital a mystery.

CITY: Danvers, Massachusetts

DATE OF FIRST REPORTED HAUNTING: unknown

TYPES OF ACTIVITY: ghost sightings, ghostly touches, footsteps, moving objects

SCARY RANKING: 4

ACCESS: There is no public access.

U.S.S. CONSTELLATION

CITY: Baltimore, Maryland

FIRST REPORTED HAUNTING: 1955

TYPES OF ACTIVITY: ghost sightings, strange smells, noises, unexplained lights

SCARY RANKING: 2

ACCESS: Public tours are available.

The U.S.S. *Constellation* was the first ship built by the U.S. Navy. First launched in 1797, the *Constellation* engaged in several battles. In 1853 the ship was taken apart, and a new ship with the same name was built. For another 100 years, the *Constellation* performed new duties. The ship brought food to Ireland during a **famine**. It was a training site for sailors during World War I (1914–1918). The *Constellation* was taken out of service in 1955. The ship is now a National Historic Landmark in Baltimore, Maryland.

Ghost sightings aboard the *Constellation* started occurring the same year it was taken out of service. Two ghosts, a sailor and a captain, have been seen roaming the decks. Visitors claim they are the ghosts of Captain Thomas Truxton and sailor Neil Harvey. In the 1700s Navy officers used harsh punishments for sailors. In 1799 Truxton ordered that sailor Harvey be killed for falling asleep on watch.

Other ghostly sightings have been reported aboard the *Constellation*. A priest once thanked staff for his well-informed tour guide. He later found out that there was no tour guide. Other visitors have seen ghostly lights and heard unexplained noises on the ship. Often the smell of gunpowder occurs before the **paranormal** events.

"One time, I switched on the alarm system, turned off all the lights and locked up for the night. The next day, the place was still locked from the inside, but the lights and a radio were on."
– James L. Hudgins, director of the U.S.S. *Constellation* in 1976

famine—a serious shortage of food resulting in widespread hunger and death
paranormal—having to do with an unexplained event

25

GOVERNOR SPRAGUE MANSION MUSEUM

CITY: Cranston, Rhode Island

FIRST REPORTED HAUNTING: 1928

TYPES OF ACTIVITY: ghost sightings, footsteps, voices, cold spots, ghostly touches

SCARY RANKING: 4

ACCESS: Open for visitors, weddings, and parties.

At first glance, the Governor Sprague Mansion Museum appears to be an old, stately home. However, its white columns and formal furnishings mask a dark past.

The Sprague Mansion began as a modest home. It was built in Cranston, Rhode Island, in the late 1700s. It takes its name from Colonel Amasa Sprague, who in the 1800s turned the house into an elegant mansion. However, Sprague was murdered on New Year's Eve in 1843. John Gordon, who worked for Sprague, was found guilty of the murder and was executed. However, later evidence suggested Gordon was not guilty.

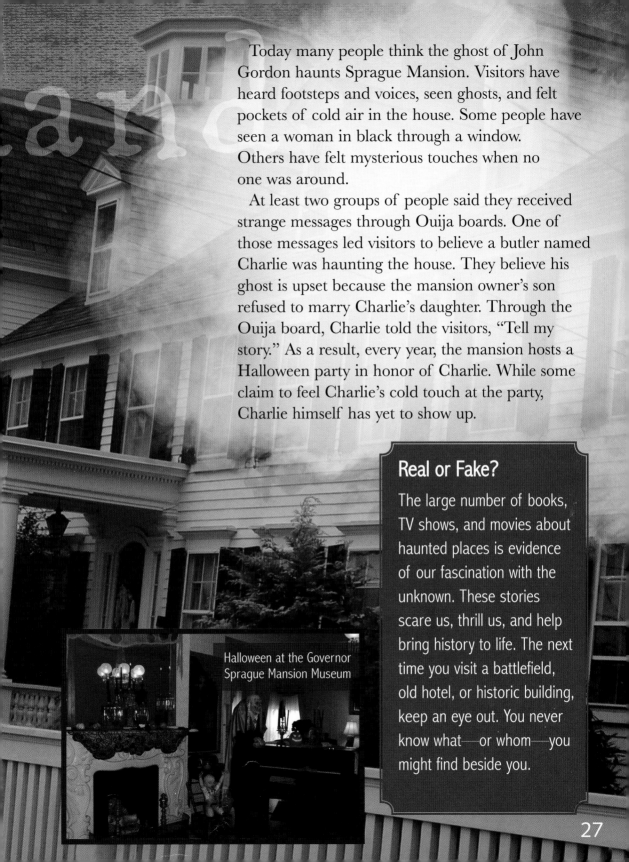

Today many people think the ghost of John Gordon haunts Sprague Mansion. Visitors have heard footsteps and voices, seen ghosts, and felt pockets of cold air in the house. Some people have seen a woman in black through a window. Others have felt mysterious touches when no one was around.

At least two groups of people said they received strange messages through Ouija boards. One of those messages led visitors to believe a butler named Charlie was haunting the house. They believe his ghost is upset because the mansion owner's son refused to marry Charlie's daughter. Through the Ouija board, Charlie told the visitors, "Tell my story." As a result, every year, the mansion hosts a Halloween party in honor of Charlie. While some claim to feel Charlie's cold touch at the party, Charlie himself has yet to show up.

Halloween at the Governor Sprague Mansion Museum

Real or Fake?

The large number of books, TV shows, and movies about haunted places is evidence of our fascination with the unknown. These stories scare us, thrill us, and help bring history to life. The next time you visit a battlefield, old hotel, or historic building, keep an eye out. You never know what—or whom—you might find beside you.

27

HAUNTED PLACES IN THIS BOOK

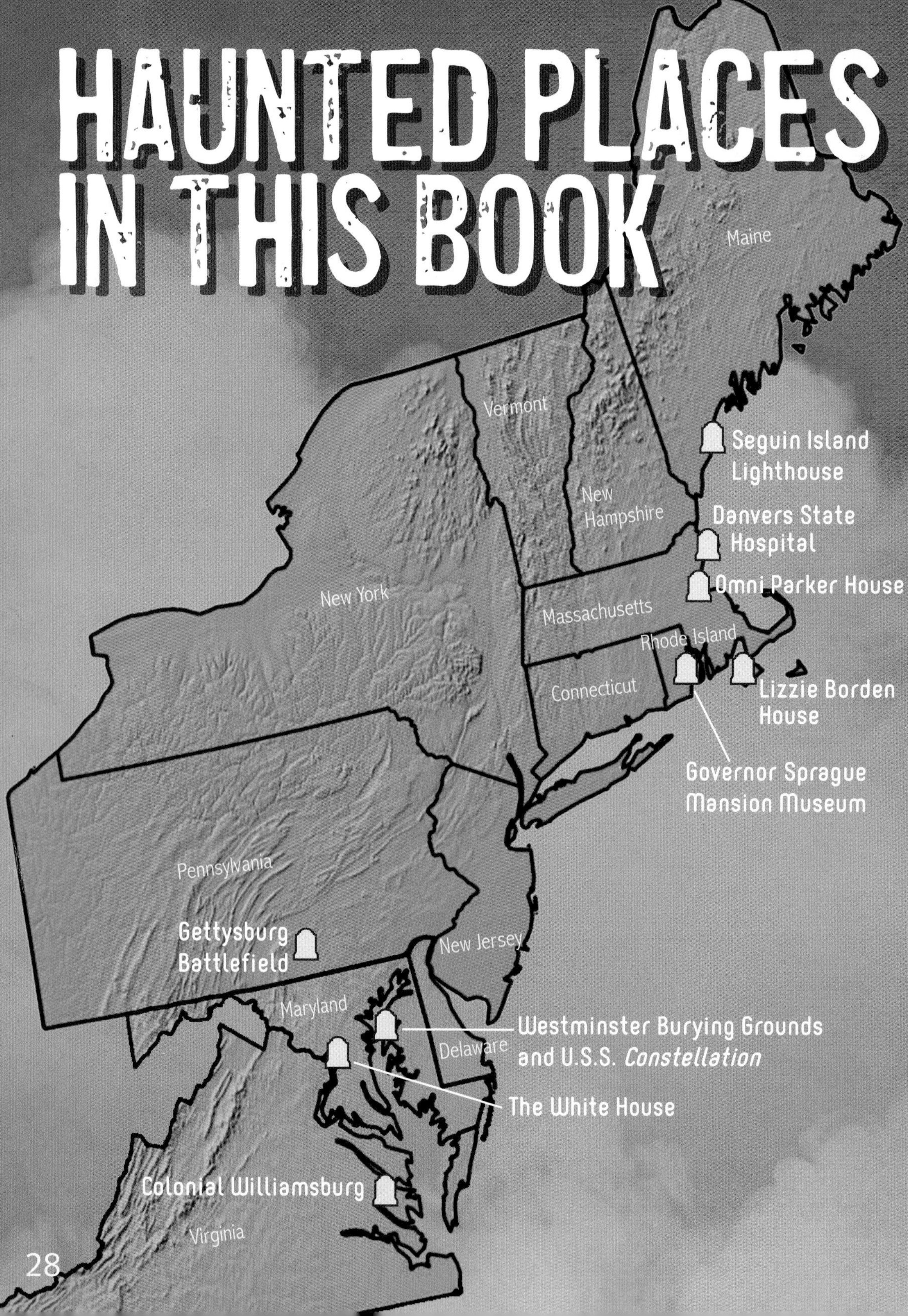

Maine

Vermont

New Hampshire

Seguin Island Lighthouse

Danvers State Hospital

Omni Parker House

New York

Massachusetts

Rhode Island

Lizzie Borden House

Connecticut

Governor Sprague Mansion Museum

Pennsylvania

Gettysburg Battlefield

New Jersey

Maryland

Westminster Burying Grounds and U.S.S. *Constellation*

Delaware

The White House

Colonial Williamsburg

Virginia

28

OTHER HAUNTED LOCATIONS OF THE EAST

The East has many other ghoulish places to explore:

- America's Stonehenge in Salem, New Hampshire
- Ice House Restaurant in Burlington, Vermont
- Fort Delaware in Delaware City, Delaware
- Roxy Studios in Long Island City, New York
- Barclay Cemetery in Leroy, Pennsylvania
- Ford's Theatre in Washington, D.C.
- Fredericksburg and Spotsylvania National Military Park, Virginia

GLOSSARY

amputate (AM-pyuh-tayt)—to cut off someone's arm, leg, or other body part

catacomb (CAT-uh-kohm)—an underground cemetery

Confederacy (kuhn-FED-ur-uh-see)—the 11 southern states that left the United States to form the Confederate States of America

famine (FA-muhn)—a serious shortage of food resulting in widespread hunger and death

inherit (in-HER-it)—to be given someone's property after they die

medium (MEE-dee-uhm)—a person who claims to communicate with the spirit world

orb (ORB)—a glowing ball of light that sometimes appears at a reportedly haunted location

paranormal (pair-uh-NOR-muhl)—having to do with an unexplained event

penitentiary (pen-uh-TEN-chur-ee)—a prison for people found guilty of serious crimes

Union (YOON-yuhn)—the northern states that fought against the Southern states in the Civil War

READ MORE

Belanger, Jeff. *The World's Most Haunted Places.* Haunted. New York: Rosen Pub., 2009.

Chandler, Matt. *The World's Most Haunted Places.* The Ghost Files. Mankato, Minn.: Capstone Press, 2012.

Everett, J.H., and Marilyn Scott-Waters. *Haunted Histories: Creepy Castles, Dark Dungeons, and Powerful Palaces.* Christy Ottaviano Books. New York: Henry Holt and Company, 2012.

INTERNET SITES

FactHound offers a safe, fun way to find Internet sites related to this book. All of the sites on FactHound have been researched by our staff.

Here's all you do:

Visit *www.facthound.com*

Type in this code: 9781476539164

Check out projects, games and lots more at
www.capstonekids.com

INDEX